PILLNITZ

AND PARK

Andrea Dietrich

Dirk Welich

Edition Leipzig

SCHLOESSERLAND SACHSEN
SAXON PALACES, CASTLES AND GARDENS

The Pillnitz Castle complex is situated several kilometres up-river from the centre of Dresden, in a picturesque spot on the right-hand bank of the Elbe. Pillnitz is one of the baroque residences that August the Strong (1670–1733) had built in and around the capital of his electorate. This pleasure estate on the Elbe surrounded by a varied garden was the summer residence of Saxony's royal house until 1918.

There has been a grand building here since 1400, and it has changed hands several times. We know that at one time during this early period it belonged to the Ziegler family, which held the estate of Pillnitz from 1486 to 1569 as a lease from the ruler. In 1569, Christoph von Loss, "des heyligen Römischen Reichs Pfennigmeister" (the treasurer of the Holy Roman Empire), was gifted the estate by Elector Christian I of Saxony (1560–1591). The lord of the manor had the Castle Church built in 1594, on a site near to the Pillnitz Neues Palais (New Palace) that we know to-

day. His son Joachim von Loss (1576–1633) went down in history as "wicked Loss" because he treated the local peasants with great rigour in his administration of the manor and in the way in which he wielded his powers as lord of the manor. Legend has it that he had to roam around the neighbourhood at midnight in the form of a large black dog, in order to howl and bark in atonement for the injustices he had committed.

It is in the 17th century that a fruit and kitchen garden are first mentioned. In 1620, a garden is mentioned "in which all kinds of fruits from the Mediterranean and elsewhere, such as figs, pomegranates, bitter oranges and laurels [...] are grown, together with all kinds of good fruits that are grown all year round: melons, artichokes and other fruits". Grapevines are also mentioned, alongside a building "in which one could shelter the foreign fruits, rosemary and other plants from frost and cold during the night". Today, we are reminded of this period by the substructure of the Löwenkopfbastei (Lion's Head

Bastion) – a pleasure building based on the pleasure building at the Dresden Jungfernbastei (Maiden Bastion).

THE MISTRESSES' CASTLE

Günther von Bünau (1604–1659) came into possession of Pillnitz in 1636 through his marriage to Sophie Sibylle, daughter of Joachim von Loss, inheriting it after her early death in 1640. He and his second wife donated the Pirna sandstone altar to the Castle Church in 1648. After the Castle Church was demolished, this altar was housed in the Weinbergkirche (Vineyard Church).

Elector Johann Georg IV (1668–1694) acquired Pillnitz from von Bünau in 1694, giving him Lichtenwalde in return. He gave the Castle and the estate to his mistress, Magdalena Sibylla von Neitschütz (1675–1694). At the time, Pillnitz was already

Riverside Palace, Castle Church and Renaissance Castle in Pillnitz. Pen drawing, 1721

Bust of August the Strong by Paul Heermann, 1718 (copy dating from 2006)

Picture of Anna Constantia, Countess of Cosel, 1715

the site of an imposing Renaissance Castle that had four wings and had replaced an older, smaller complex. The original manor was gradually expanded to create a building with four separate wings. A lodge (a residential building) was added in the 17th century, with the clock and stair towers and the roof gables as the most striking elements.

After the early deaths of Johann Georg IV and his mistress in the year 1694, Pillnitz came into the possession of the elector's younger brother, who became Elector Friedrich August I of Saxony and subsequently (in 1697) August II, King of Poland. He is remembered in the history of Saxony as August the Strong. In 1707, he in his turn bestowed the estate on a mistress: Countess Anna Constantia of Cosel (1680–1765). The Countess Cosel used the Castle as a summer resi-

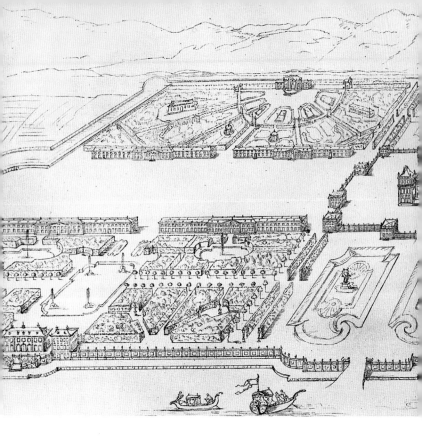

"Grand Plan" of the castle and garden in Pillnitz. Drawing, 1720/21. The Plan was not implemented.

dence, and laid out a garden there. She had the labyrinth-like hornbeam hedge gardens known as the Charmillen planted. Although the hornbeam hedges that are in place today do not date back to this period, the structure of these modern hedges derives from the same plan. After a liaison lasting eight years, the countess fell into disfavour. August ordered her to leave the court and to remain in Pillnitz, once the scene of pleasant summers. Eventually, she was imprisoned at Stolpen. August took back Pillnitz in 1718. From this time forth, Pillnitz was no longer a leased

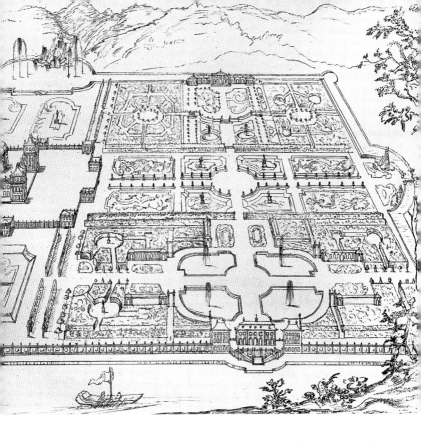

estate, but remained in the possession of the state's rulers.

1720 saw the beginning of an intensive phase of construction activity at Pillnitz. The basic structure of the complex that we see today dates from this period. It represented the realisation of a dream long cherished by the Castle's master. A "grand plan" for Pillnitz dating from 1720/21 shows what was envisioned. A square central building sits amid an extended garden complex, magnificent, but also quite inhuman in its scale; only small parts of this ambitious project could be realised in the end. The grand tour August the Strong undertook as a young

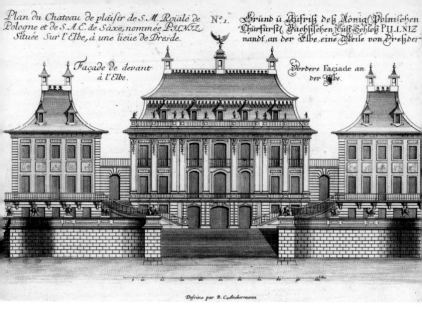

Plan of the Riverside Palace by Alexander Glässer, circa 1730

opposite
Vineyard "Church of the Holy Spirit" on the slope above the Pillnitz Castle complex

prince took him through France and Italy, where the city of Venice's waterside location, palaces and lavish carnivals clearly made an impression on him. Why not turn the Elbe into the Canal Grande? As the royal city of Dresden was still a fortress and could therefore not be opened up to the Elbe, he applied this plan to castles and palaces up and down the Elbe. Übigau Castle, the Japanese Palace and the Pillnitz Pleasure Garden were opened up to the river. In Pillnitz, a grand staircase led to a waterside palace on the Elbe where gondola-type river boats built for the purpose of royal outings, could tie up. August dreamed of an "Indian pleasure palace" here on the banks of the Elbe, and commissioned chief architect Matthäus Daniel Pöppelmann (1662–1736) to build it for him.

Pöppelmann was born in Herford in Westphalia and had lived in Dresden since 1668. He had already distinguished himself with the Dresden Zwinger building. He succeeded Johann Friedrich Karcher (1650–1726) as chief architect for the state of Saxony in 1718. He had already had a hand in the design of the Japanese Palace, and while Pillnitz was under construction he worked on conversions at Grosssedlitz, Moritzburg and Graditz. The first phase of construction (from 1720 to 1730) saw the building of the two "twin palaces" on the Elbe and on the Borsberg slope, known respectively as the Wasserpalais (Riverside Palace) and the Bergpalais (Upper Palace). Pöppelmann also planned the grand open-air staircase leading to the Elbe (1724), the Church of the Holy Spirit, which is also known as the Vineyard Church (1723–1725), and the Temple of Venus (1725), a grand octagonal building that served as a banqueting and festive hall. From 1724 onwards, Pöppelmann was assisted by Zacharias Longue-

lune (1669–1748), who arrived in Dresden in 1713 and was quickly appointed as court architect by August the Strong. Longuelune's characteristic style was heavily influenced by classicist French baroque. The old Castle Church was removed to make way for the Temple of Venus, which was to house a gallery of the court of Poland and Saxony's greatest beauties. Pöppelmann was then commissioned to build a new and Protestant church for Pillnitz – the Vineyard Church. Some accoutrements – such as the Bünau altar – were transferred from the older church and are still housed in the Vineyard Church today. This altar was restored to its former glory when the Vineyard Church was renovated in the 1990s. The great castle garden, with its rows of lime and horse chestnut trees (now extremely old) was laid out behind the Upper Palace during this period.

COURT AMUSEMENTS AND A SUMMER RESIDENCE

The two palace buildings and the old Renaissance Castle to the east represented a kind of royal court; they were used by August the Strong as a venue for his entertainments. Many of his castles were reserved for a particular purpose: just as Moritzburg was his hunting lodge and the meetings of the Polish Order of the White Eagle were held at Grosssedlitz, Pillnitz Castle hosted court amusements.

Pillnitz became the summer residence of the royal house of Wettin in 1765. Because the existing buildings were not adequate to keep the court in comfort over a longer period of time, a second period of design was

embarked upon, followed by another phase of intensive construction activity. Elector Friedrich Au-
gust III (1750–1827) gave orders for the Pillnitz Castle
complex to be significantly extended, and the wooden
buildings on either side of the Upper Palace and the
Riverside Palace were replaced by classicist buildings based
on plans by Christian Traugott Weinlig (1739–1799) and Johann Daniel Schade (1730–1798), with Christian Friedrich
Exner (1718–1798) supervising the construction work. In
the year 1791, Pillnitz was the scene of the meeting of
heads of state at which the Pillnitz Declaration, a measure
directed against the French revolutionaries, was drawn up.

Friedrich August III was a passionate collector of
beautiful and rare plants, and the Pillnitz gardens were
extended at his behest. The so-called English Garden (a
landscape garden in the new English style, complete with
the English Pavilion) was created in 1778, and the Dutch
Garden was created in 1785. The latter included a botanical nursery, with greenhouses and beds for raising plants

Friedrich August I of Saxony (1750–1827) was the longest-reigning ruler of Saxony in history, and the first King of Saxony. His father, Elector Friedrich Christian (1722–1763), died when he was a young prince of 13 years of age, after having reigned only a few weeks, and his son duly succeeded him as Elector Friedrich August III. Because he had not yet reached the age of majority, his uncle, Prince Xaver of Saxony (1730–1806), governed until 1768. Friedrich August III was highly active in rebuilding his domain, which had suffered extensive losses in the Seven Years' War, and Saxony's economy was substantially strengthened during his rule.

The alliance of the electors with Napoleon was to have dramatic consequences for Saxony. To accede to demands from Prussia, Friedrich August III's armies initially fought against Napoleon, but when defeat appeared imminent for Napoleon's opponents, he changed sides by joining the Confederation of the Rhine, under the leadership of Napoleon. The Elector of Saxony was accorded the title of king by the Treaty of Posen, signed in December 1806. Now a king thanks to Napoleon's support, he took the name Friedrich August I. This increase in status obliged Friedrich August to contribute soldiers for the French emperor's campaigns. The ruler remained faithful to his pact with France, and was at Napoleon's side in the devastating defeat of the Battle of Nations at Leipzig in October 1813. The outcome of the Congress of Vienna, imposed by the victors, was a humiliation for the defeated Saxony. The captured king

Picture of Friedrich August the Just, 1792

was forced to give up two thirds of his territory to Prussia. He returned to a much-reduced kingdom in 1815.

Friedrich August I was noted for a strong adherence to justice, which earned him the epithet "the Just". As an older man, however, he refused to undertake the urgently necessary political reforms that were eventually implemented by his nephew, King Friedrich August II (1797–1854). The first King of Saxony died in 1827, having reigned for almost six decades. He married Maria Amalie Auguste von Zweibrücken-Birkenfeld-Bischweiler (1752–1828), who bore him four children: three stillbirths and a daughter who remained unmarried. As a result, the succession passed to his brother Anton (1755–1836) and subsequently – because his younger brother Maximilian (1759–1838) declined the offer of kingship – to his nephew Friedrich August II.

Friedrich August I and Friedrich August II were both passionate amateur botanists and plant collectors. An interest in rare plants and their classification was widespread among the European ruling houses of the age, from St. Petersburg to Paris. Friedrich August I, however, practiced botany himself as well as promoting the science. He was assisted by Ludwig Reichenbach (1793–1879), founder of Dresden's Botanical Gardens and, as of 1820, director of the Royal Natural History Museum in Dresden. The king was energetic in exchanging ideas with scientists. He kept botanical novelties that were presented to him and collected them in a greenhouse and in a herbarium that he created personally. From 1785 onwards, Friedrich August I had drawings made of rare plants. Court botanical painters were engaged to perform this task for over four decades, and were instructed in the correct dissection of blossoms and fruits by the king himself. The "Pillnitzer Centurien", ten magnificent volumes containing 1,000 drawings of plant species that were grown at Pillnitz, survives today to bear impressive witness to this. It was created at the behest of Friedrich August II, who also took a keen interest in botany. His excursions in the environs of Dresden and travels through Europe gave him the opportunity to complete his uncle's herbarium. The treatises "Flora von Dresden" and "Flora von Marienbad" were the result of his collecting and categorising of plants. Whereas Friedrich August I presided over the creation of the English Garden, Chinese Garden, Dutch Garden and Botanical Nursery, Friedrich August II devoted particular care to the Castle Botanical Gardens. In the reign of King Johann (1801–1873), the areas of the Castle Park complex occupied by the botanical collection's plant specimens were altered, and the era of scientific plant husbandry at Pillnitz came to an end.

(used until 1867). Today, the Pillnitz plant collections continue to be an important feature of the gardens. During the summer months, the Castle Park contains around 600 tub plants – one of the largest and oldest plant collections of its kind in Germany.

In 1785, a structure was built on the extended line of the Upper Palace's central axis. Constructed high above the Friedrichsgrund (the natural continuation of the English Garden into the open landscape towards the Borsberg), this artificial Gothic ruin was situated on a site believed to have been the location for a second "old Castle" according to a plan dating back to the 16th century.

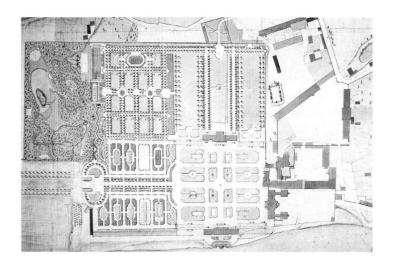

Overview of Pillnitz Castle and Park (detail), 1780

opposite

Citrus tree planted in tub in the Pillnitz Castle Park

By 1790, the gardens had attained their modern dimensions, with the creation of the Chinese Garden and of the pavilion of the same name located within it.

The old Renaissance Castle and the Temple of Venus burned to the ground on the 1st of May 1818. The Stände-versammlung (Estates Assembly) immediately granted the ruler 60,000 talers for the purposes of rebuilding the summer residence. The exterior work was completed by 1826. This third phase of building gave the castle a suitably impressive east face. Friedrich August I of Saxony, who acquired the title of "King" in 1806, commissioned Christian Friedrich Schuricht (1753–1832) to build the so-called New Palace, a three-winged complex. Its more well-preserved rooms include the southern kichen wing that housed the Royal Court Kitchen and the Catholic Chapel (consecrated in 1830) in the northern chapel wing. The New Palace incorporates the Lilac Courtyard,

The Pillnitz declaration

In 1791, the previously tranquil estate of Pillnitz was the scene of an event of global political significance. Leopold II (1747–1792), Joseph II's successor as Holy Roman Emperor, and King Friedrich Wilhelm II of Prussia (1744–1797) met with Elector Friedrich August III of Saxony (1750–1827) on the neutral ground of Pillnitz to discuss a number of questions of world politics. The Polish question was discussed (the Elector of Saxony had recently been offered the crown of Poland) and an end to the Austria–Ottoman Empire war was debated. Ultimately, Leopold II and Friedrich Wilhelm II acceded to demands from the Count of Artois, who was later to become King Charles X of France (1757–1836), to institute measures against the French revolutionaries. The agreement provided for military action, but only if all major powers were in unanimous agreement: the reluctance of Great Britain therefore made it improbable that any military action would take place. This rather half-hearted declaration nonetheless provided the radical faction of the revolutionary party with a welcome justification for accelerating the pace of the revolution. As a consequence of this, when he visited Pillnitz in the year 1812, Napoleon reportedly declared: "I was born here!"

The meeting of rulers in 1791 saw Pillnitz once again become the backdrop for a celebration lasting several days, with lavish operas and ballets and extravagant banquets in the Temple of Venus. The buildings at Pillnitz were magnificently illuminated, and the celebrations concluded with a firework display. Although the Declaration of Pillnitz did not ease tensions between Prussia and Austria or resolve the Polish question, it is remembered in history as an imposing display of a ruler's power.

which was created in 1828. Its highlight is the festival and dining hall in the central tract, which is linked to the Riverside Palace and the Upper Palace by arched galleries. This hall is believed to be the only classicist domed building in Dresden. Like the chapel, it was painted by court painter Carl Christian Vogel von Vogelstein (1788–1868). The castle structure as we see it today was completed during the tenure of King Anton (1755–1836), who ruled jointly with his nephew Friedrich August II (1797–1854).

opposite

Palm house in the Dutch Garden, 1885

BIEDERMEIER PILLNITZ

In the first half of the 19th century, during the tenure of the aesthetically-minded Prince Johann (1801–1873, subsequently King of Saxony), the cheerful estate of Pillnitz became an ideal location for scintillating intellectual debate. Johann would hold readings at which he would present translations of verses from Dante's Divine Comedy (signed with the pseudonym "Philaletes") to a select circle of thinkers. At the meetings of the "Academia Dantesca", which presumably took place in the Chinese Pavilion, he discussed these translations with authorities such as the author Ludwig Tieck (1773–1853), the physician and painter Carl Gustav Carus (1789–1869), professor of literature Carl Förster (1784–1841) and art historian Carl Friedrich von Rumohr (1785–1843). The end result – his commentary on

Narrow-leaved Pitcairnia from the "Pillnitzer Centurien", pre-1795

the Divine Comedy – is still highly regarded by academics today.

The presence of the court – and also the stimulating intellectual atmosphere, the pleasant and almost Mediterranean landscape and the favourable climate created at Pillnitz by the Borsberg, which blocks cold northerly winds – led to many artists, court officials and wealthy private individuals either settling at Pillnitz or spending their summers there during the 19th century. Today, the summer homes of Carl Maria von Weber (1786–1826) at Hosterwitz, Richard Wagner (1813–1883) in the adjacent locality of Graupa and Carl Gustav Carus in Pillnitz are visitor and gastronomic destinations.

The reign of King Johann saw the construction of more botanical facilities for the care of valuable plants at Pillnitz. The Palm House was constructed between 1859 and 1861 on the former site of the Botanical Nursery. It is a cast iron-and-glass structure that was highly advanced when it was built and is today considered the oldest surviving building of its kind in Germany. Restored and restocked with plants in 2009, it is now open to visitors, primarily as a winter attraction. The symmetrical flowerbeds that were laid out during the construction of the

Palm House can also be seen. Today, the Palm House contains plants from South Africa, New Zealand and Australia. Among other exotic plants, Proteaceae, Strelitzia, Gerbera and, of course, palm trees flourish on the 660 square metres of space within, even in the winter.

The central Pleasure Garden as we know it today was created in 1867, by Peter Joseph Lenné (1789–1866) and others. The flower terrace to the north of the Great Castle Garden was also redesigned at this time. The statue of Flora by the sculptor Wolf von Hoyer (1806–1873) was erected circa 1870. The extension buildings on the 'Ringrennen' building facing towards the Orangerie (*Ringrennen* refers to the sport of tilting at rings) were constructed in 1874 during the rule of King Albert of Saxony (1828–1902), the son and successor of Johann. At around this time, the Games Garden was redesigned and turned into a conifer grove. This work was completed in 1880. The exceptional dendrological specimens in this area of the park, which include many plants from North America, have been growing here for 100 years, so that we can see them today in their full glory.

FROM RESIDENCE TO MUSEUM

Pillnitz continued to be the summer residence of the Wettin royal house until the end of the First World War and the abdication of King Friedrich August III (1865–1932). In 1924, the whole complex passed into the possession of the state. It became the site of artists' apartments and workshops, and from 1924 public tours allowed interested visitors to view the rooms.

Pillnitz Castle was one of the few Dresden public buildings to escape destruction during the Second World War. As a result, it served as a place to bring together and take stock of the evacuated art objects from Dresden's world-famous collections. These art objects were subsequently transported to the Soviet Union. In 1946, the Soviet military administration ordered the "Zentralmuseum im Bundesland Sachsen" or "central museum in the federal state of Saxony" to be set up at Pillnitz to house pictures and other works of art that now had no home in the destroyed city centre (until the rebuilding of the Sempergalerie and the Albertinum). The Kunstgewerbemuseum der Staatlichen Kunstsammlungen Dresden (the arts and crafts museum of the Dresden state art collections) was opened in 1963, and is still housed in the Riverside Palace and in the Upper Palace today. The Castle Museum in the New Palace has existed to inform visitors about the construction and history of the castle and its gardens since 2006.

The redesign of individual parts of the gardens during the 1950s was supervised by the city of Dresden, which took on the gardens in 1952 following the dissolution of the state of Saxony. A small collection of conifers was accumulated, and the once empty hedge gardens are today adorned by rose and perennial gardens. In 1993, the castle and its park were restored to the Free State of Saxony. The "Palaces and Gardens in Dresden", including Pillnitz, are now part of the group "State Palaces, Castles and Gardens in Saxony".

In addition to the 28 hectares of gardens, the vineyards (replanted in the 1980s), the Vineyard Church and the Pillnitz Elbe island (a conservation site, situated close to the Riverside Palace) are part of the historic ensemble

View of the Riverside Palace from the Pleasure Garden side

today. Amongst other things, the Elbe island was once used to raise the royal pheasants. Today, it is a unique natural site, with rare alluvial forest plants and nesting sites of a number of bird species.

THE RIVERSIDE PALACE AND THE UPPER PALACE

The Riverside Palace (1) and the Upper Palace (2) are the two oldest surviving structures at Pillnitz. The Riverside Palace was formerly the site of a pleasure building dating back to 1720. A number of extensions created two symmetrical palace buildings on the edge of the Pleasure Garden. Their current integration into the overall plan was not a feature of the original plan conceived by August the

Strong for his pleasure estate on the Elbe, which foresaw a castle with four wings and a central tower with a dome and four corner towers in the centre of an estate four times the size of the Pillnitz we know surrounded by nine grand houses. In this design, the castle was surrounded by extensive baroque gardens with ponds, boskets (areas planted with trees and bushes and surrounded by hedges) and hedge gardens. This original plan – the so-called Grand Plan – was born out of the need for calculated ostentation common to absolutist rulers such as August the Strong, whose high-level power political machinations saw him crowned King of Poland and Grand Duke of Lithuania in 1697. Pillnitz was to be merely one of 24 variously themed pleasure estates situated along the Elbe, intended to embody the power and nobility of the ruler. The palace buildings that were actually built were to have been merely the gates to the Elbe waterfront and to the hillside landscape.

As it turned out, the implementation was rather more modest than the plan. Three free-standing pavilions were built on the Elbe side and the hillside respectively, creating the Riverside Palace and the Upper Palace of today. The connective passages that unite the structures were created at a later date. The pavilions were never intended for residential purposes: instead, they were gates that formed the prelude to the gardens – the actual venue for the amusements.

August the Strong wished Pillnitz to be built in the "ginetisch" (Chinese) style, and the architect Matthäus Daniel Pöppelmann (who both created the design and oversaw its implementation) complied with this requirement by creating curving roofs. Pöppelmann was inspired by the group of structures constituting the throne hall in

The Watteau Room in the Upper Palace

the emperor's palace in Peking, known to him through contemporary etchings. This three-part group of pavilions is therefore analogous to the throne hall group in shape. Despite being European inventions, the concave curve of the roof gutters and the figurative *chinoiserie* scenes also serve to give the castle the intended effect. The Oriental atmosphere is also reinforced by the way the courtyard-facing sides of the central pavilion (which is based on the Trianon de Porcelaine in the park of Versailles) are painted. Built by Louis XIV (1638–1715) as a private retreat for his mistress, Madame de Montespan, the Trianon de Porcelaine imitated the Tower of Nanking, which is covered entirely in porcelain. Like the emperor's throne hall, this porcelain tower was known to Europeans through etchings, with European rulers seeking to emulate this marvel in order to emphasise their own impor-

tance. August's architect, however, was well-travelled as well as being a capable producer of exotic ornamentation, making it unsurprising that the pavilions facing the courtyard have the structural division and colonnaded fronts of Palladian villas belonging to Italian landed gen-

try, whilst the façade that faces onto the Elbe is reminiscent of palaces in the lagoon city of Venice.

With the exception of the fireplaces, the interiors of the two palace buildings contain few elements dating from this early period. The appearance they present today largely dates from the late 19th century. The main hall

Pillnitz Castle is among the most large-scale and significant examples of this fashion for Chinese decoration. Chinoiserie – an 18th-century term derived from the French word chinois (Chinese) – describes a stylistic phenomena inspired by Far East culture in general and by China in particular that exerted an influence for over three centuries, extending to the early 20th century. Its manifestations were variable, permeated multiple artistic genres and often involved the mixing of artforms. For almost the whole of the time during which this East Asian influence was prevalent, Pillnitz Castle was among its most exemplary reflections.

When this fashion for borrowing from the Far East first began, no distinction was made between the art of China, Japan and India. Instead, the non-differentiated term "indianisch" (Indian) was used, and was generally understood to mean a fantastic realm located far to the east. Mental images of this realm were based more on the impressions gained from typical Asiatic wares such as porcelain, silk and lacquered goods and from projected yearnings and fantasies than on real knowledge. This meant that the image that the Europeans of the time had of the East Asian world was rather like a myth – and, as a myth, it was subject to being interpreted in a variety of ways to serve different interests.

The chinoiserie mythos generated fabricated "Chinese" paintings and other imitations of Chinese or East Asian art forms, East Asian products to suit European tastes and European designs with original East Asian elements integrated into them. Crucially, the designs created an impression of being unknown and exotically foreign, making them open to interpretation. This also made chinoiserie very suitable for politically-motivated ostentation by absolutist rulers in the 17th and 18th centuries – to a certain extent it even epitomised the artistic equivalent of their absolutist power.

Chinoiserie wall painting on the portico of the Upper Palace

The Yellow Tea Room in the Riverside Palace

of the Upper Palace is particularly striking. Its creation in 1890 was the first act in a new wave of *chinoiserie* at Pillnitz. There are definite signs of a Japanese influence (Japan opened its ports to trade in 1854, resulting in large numbers of Japanese art objects arriving in Europe). The paintings extend across all the room's fixtures including the ceiling, suggesting that the pictorial source material was highly complex. The character of the source drawings, however, shows that there were no content connections between the sequence of painted subjects. The room displays decorative representations of plants alongside emblematic or symbolic animal and figural representations and narrative genre scenes. Given that Chinese figurative influences are also present, one cannot describe the main hall as an authentic design in the Japanese style – it is simply a fantasy engendered by the diversity of styles prevalent in the 19th century. What is known as the Watteau Gallery is a salon in the neo-rococo style created by the sculptor Emil Schäfer in 1882. The wall panels, which date from the latter part of the 18th century, probably came from the workshop of court painter Christian Wilhelm Dietrich (1712–1774). Painted in the style of Antoine Watteau (1684–1721), the pastoral scenes are reminiscent of the era of court celebrations at Pillnitz, and suggest how their more intimate scenes were played out in the Pleasure Garden.

Under Georg of Saxony (1832–1904), who succeeded to the throne in 1902, the Riverside Palace was redesigned as part of the royal summer residence. The Hofbaurat (court architecture official) Gustav Frölich (1859–1933) was responsible for creating the Yellow Tearoom. This room was also in the neo-rococo style. The ornamental shapes, with their colour scheme of yellow and white, are entirely in the spirit of rococo. Figural Chinese scenes on the themes of games, dance, pleasure rambles and hunting are surrounded by extravagant curving shapes embellished with exotic birds and dragons. The room's stucco decorations extend to parts of the furniture – the large mirrors in the form of Asiatic heads, for instance. Remarkably, the furniture and porcelain for the room was also chosen with the wall designs in mind. Despite this unity of design, however, the room is very much in the *chinoiserie* style – which, like the baroque style, had a rather distorted view of the Far East.

opposite
Computer model view of the Castle complex as it
appeared in the mid-18th century

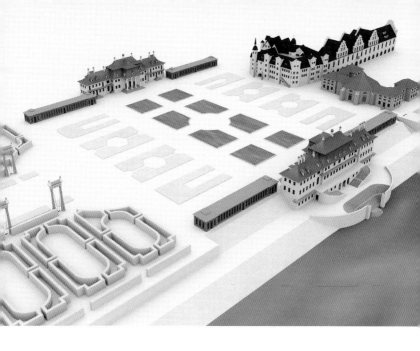

THE PLEASURE GARDEN AND OTHER VENUES FOR COURT AMUSEMENTS

The **Pleasure Garden** (3) extends from the Riverside Palace to the Upper Palace. In the first half of the 18th century, wooden playing galleries where court society would pursue the pleasant occupation of board games from time to time were still to be seen where the wings of the Riverside Palace and the Upper Palace are located now – a feature appropriate to Pillnitz's character as a pleasure retreat. The objects that have survived attest to a wide variety of games although few are still known to us today: these include draughts, Nine Man Morris, chess and solitaire. Other games included Chinese chess, Gänsespiel ("goose

The 18th-century höfisches Spiel (court entertainment) was a ceremony combining liturgical, musical and dramatic elements. It also, however, reflected the hierarchy of the baroque court. Despite the impression of good cheer and apparent informality, this coming together of court society for the purpose of amusement was always governed by strict social rules. For the inhabitants of the court, these entertainments were not just amusements, but also an instrument for attracting favourable attention and for achieving advancement. Participation was a required social duty, and could bring a rise or decline in fortunes. Court entertainments were held in Dresden and in the surrounding pleasure palaces – in the salons and games rooms, but particularly in the gardens. They were inspired by events at the court of Versailles, although at Pillnitz dance and ballet played a less prominent role than in France. There were a number of exceptional occasions when these festivities had a wider political importance that brought Pillnitz to national prominence: the marriages of 1719 (Prince Elector Friedrich August and Maria Josepha, daughter of Emperor Joseph I), 1725 (Augusta Constantia of Cosel to Count Heinrich Friedrich of Friesen), 1738 (Princess Maria Amalia of Saxony to King Charles III of Sicily) and 1747 (Princess Maria Anna of Saxony to Elector of Bavaria Maximilian III Joseph and his sister Princess Maria Antonia of Bavaria to the Saxon prince elector Friedrich Christian) and the founding of the royal Polish Order of the White Eagle in 1723. Aside from these special occasions, the elector and his court would hawk for wood grouse and heron at Pillnitz every year in spring. They would also celebrate August Friedrich's name day on the 5th of March, his birthday on the 12th of March, a four-day shooting festival in the middle of April, a "peasant wedding" in summer, a waterfowl hunt in September and the grape harvest and associated festival on the 2nd of November.

The design of the Pleasure Garden and the neighbouring Charmillen was determined entirely by the requirements of games and entertainments. The Ringrenngen building, for instance, the central section of the Orangerie today, was built to contain a carousel with wooden horses and carts mounted on it so that, in a simple variant of the knightly tournament, the ladies of the court could try to thrust lances through suspended wooden rings. The part of the gardens behind the Upper Palace was also used exclusively for games during the 18th century. The lawn was originally used as a shooting range, with a shooting house directly adjoining the palace and a grotto serving as the targets. Later, it served as a riding area. The parallel corridors were reserved for the Ramasse-spiel, which was played on a sort of slide.

game"), "die königliche Eichel" ("royal acorn") and *biribi*. At this time Pillnitz had a number of other leisure areas that do not survive today, but which were characteristic of the

estate's appearance at the time. For instance, between 1726 and 1750, there were ten frameworks for swings (large enough to be visible from a distance) on the part of the Maillebahn nearest Hoster-witz, at the entrance to the "Charmillen". (Charmillen was the name for the hornbeam hedge gardens laid out by the Countess Cosel as places to socialise out of doors af-ter August the Strong gave Pillnitz to her in 1707; these small courtly spaces were largely devoted to tête à têtes between ladies and cavaliers.) Sports available in the Charmillen included bowls, seesaws and a building con-structed specially for *jeu de passe*, whilst the part of the Pleasure Garden between the two palaces contained playing fields for ballgames. The games played in the Pleasure Garden included *billard-maille*, a smaller-scale variant of *paille maille*, a kind of golf in which a wooden ball is propelled over a course, Jesuiter Ring, a game in-volving running with the ball inside an iron ring, requir-

View down the Maillebahn towards Hosterwitz

ing agility, *jeu de portiques* (a game rather like roulette in which the outcome was determined by the course of a ball released in an arcade) and *La corbeille*, an early, courtly form of basketball.

The Pleasure Garden underwent a number of changes prior to its restoration and redesign in the 1940s and 1950s. Redesigned in a rococo style under Elector Friedrich August III in 1765, it first came under the influence of landscape gardening in the early 19th century.

This is demonstrated by one feature that still survives today: the joining-together of two hedged areas to create a
family garden with a private, secluded character. Between
1864 and the Second World War, the Pleasure Garden was
altered continually. It received the basic structure it still
retains today, which was based on plans by Peter Joseph
Lenné and Gustav Krause (1821–1895), in 1867. With
some exceptions, the trees planted in the Pleasure Garden also date from this period, meaning that the large
trees that we see today are over 140 years old. The flower-

The Triton Gondola in front of Pillnitz Castle.
Engraving by Christian August Günther, circa 1800

opposite top
The Triton Gondola in the Hedge Garden

opposite bottom
View of an avenue through the hornbeam hedges

bed terraces added to the garden in the late 19th century were reinstated during its post-war reconstruction.

The course for large-scale *paille maille* games, which stretched from the Pleasure Garden to the ha-ha and was enclosed by a frame made from long planks when in use, was located on the main path through the Charmillen. The Maillebahn (4) of today extends as far as Hosterwitz (its length was chosen based on the historical game). Pillnitz' gardens are enclosed by a Ha-ha (5) – a feature often seen in estate gardens. This ditch, unexpectedly inserted into the landscape, encloses the garden, but is not visible as one looks out over the Maillebahn, thereby preserving the impression of distance. The ditch only becomes visible as a barrier when one draws close to it – an

effect that often causes people to exclaim "aha". The Guard Houses (6) directly next to the ha-ha were built in the mid-19th century. They provided official residences for the castle managers.

A gondola under a protective roof has been located in the Hedge Garden since 1935. The Triton Gondola (7), which has been restored several times, gives the impression that it is carrying the court upriver from the Dresden Residence Palace to Pillnitz. It was created from two gondolas dating from around 1800, created by master shipwright Johann Christian Pätzold based on designs by Christian Friedrich Schuricht. Mounted on the bow is a triton blowing into a conch. The pavilion is decorated with festoons and with the royal coat of arms.

The gondola is a reminder of August the Strong's dream of creating a "Venice on the Elbe". The elector and king had a number of sloops or gondolas built according to the Venetian model, including a grand gondola based upon the Doge of Venice's barge. When his son, the future Elector Friedrich August II (1696–1763) was married to the emperor's daughter Maria Josepha of Austria (1699–1757) in the year 1719, a "Venetian" pleasure boat on the Elbe featured in the couple's arrival. Once the gondola harbour and its open-air staircase leading to Pillnitz Castle's Riverside Palace were completed, the court travelled to the royal city of Dresden in sloops. The red and blue boats were manned by both Italian and German gondoliers.

The Wings (8) were created during the second major phase of construction between 1788 and 1791, after Elector Friedrich August III, who later became the first King of Saxony, chose the pleasure estate of Pillnitz as his summer residence. This gave rise to a need to add buildings that were suitable for court ceremonies. To make the wing buildings consistent with the overall profile of the castle, Christian Traugott Weinlig and Johann Daniel Schade combined the classicist building style with *chinoiserie* elements.

Supraport painting in the Upper Palace bedroom, showing Eros and Psyche

The rooms – the first and second antechamber, the salon, the bedchamber and the adjoining small gallery – were arranged in the classical enfilade, with the connective doors all lying on an axis. The court ceremonies that principally governed life at court stated that courtiers were admitted to these rooms depending on their status and favour with the ruler, with the level of prestige associated with each room reflected in the relative grandeur of its décor. Only those favoured by the monarch to the highest degree were allowed to enter the small gallery. The two wings are examples of this kind of room sequence. The northwest wing of the Upper Palace is known as the imperial wing – a name that is to be taken literally, as it was occupied by Emperor Leopold II (1747–1792) during the "Pillnitzer Konvention" in 1791.

The salon and the bedchamber are highlights of the room sequence. The architect Christian Traugott Weinlig created them in a Pompeian-Egyptian style prior to the *Monarchentreffen* or meeting of heads of state in Pillnitz.

The elements he used denote a transition from rococo to classicism. The rooms' walls and supraportals are lavishly decorated with arabesques, reliefs and murals. The salon has white-golden stucco decorations on a beige-coloured background with integrated Wedgwood porcelain reliefs, while the wall sections in the neighbouring bedchamber have arabesque and pendant plant decorations in white-painted wood on a light-blue background. The exterior of the monarch's private apartments, of course, also had to be visibly grand. Because the central position was already occupied by the Riverside Palace and the Upper Palace, the prestige of the wing structures had to be increased by deploying architectural elements that betokened a high status. Christian Friedrich Exner responded to this problem with a classical temple motif. He did, however, borrow the curved roof element (which he rested on a classicist colonnade front) and the division of the structure from Pöppelmann. Each wing consists of two pavilions joined by a connective structure: this division is subtle, but can be recognized by means of the double pillars that offer an easy transition to the slightly recessed central section, and the pavilions' separate roof ridges.

Two-storey round arches provide an architectural connection between the new wing buildings and the two *Palais*, in both structural groups. Until the restoration at the end of the 1990s, the side facing the Elbe had light and airy superstructures made from loadbearing wrought-iron scaffolds clad with timber and with a row of windows. Erected in the early 19th century, these roofing elements attested to the relaxing of court ceremony – the members of court society who lodged in the upper storey were no longer forced to pass through the outdoor space in order to reach the social rooms in the *Palais*.

THE NEW PALACE AND THE LILAC COURTYARD

After a major fire on the 1st of May 1818, which completely destroyed the Altes Schloss (the old castle) and the Temple of Venus, chief state architect Christian Friedrich Schuricht was required to create a new structure to replace the functional areas of the castle complex that had been lost without destroying the overall harmony of the complex. The New Palace (9) was built between 1818 and 1826, based on his plans. Schuricht satisfied architectonic requirements by emulating the *chinoiserie* design concept originated by Pöppelmann and by retaining the complex's basic structure and divisions: pavilions and connective structures, combined with curved roofs. The superimposed Corinthian columns of the central structure echo the use of columns in the Riverside Palace and the Upper Palace, whilst the colonnade front of the corner pavilions

echoes that of the pre-existing wing structures. Schuricht included the clock tower and the attic on the Pleasure Garden façade as references to the appearance of the old Renaissance Castle, whose roof was decorated with gables and a tower.

From the Pleasure Garden, an open staircase leads to the large glazed doors between the columns, which open onto the Kuppelsaal (Domed Hall). The Kapellenflügel or chapel wing adjoins the central, main tract of the New Palace to the east, on the side facing the Borsberg, whereas the kitchen wing adjoins it on the side facing the Elbe. The Domed Hall, built to serve as a dining hall, is at the heart of the New Palace. Built in the 1820s as a venue for events requiring pomp and prestige, it is a classicist domed structure that receives abundant light. It is built on a square floor plan, and its roof is a wide, coffered dome supported on all sides by an unbroken column structure with a classical entablature. Its construction alone is a masterpiece, as the concave curve of the roof left very little space in which to construct its dome. Taken together, the palace kitchen (situated in the basement) the Domed Hall and its adjoining service rooms are a very effective functional unit.

The hall's painted decorations are also exceptional. They were created by Carl Christian Vogel von Vogelstein (1788–1868), who was appointed professor of the Royal Art Academy in Dresden in 1820 and was appointed painter to the royal court in 1824. Originally from Wildenfels near Zwickau and raised to the nobility by decree, he worked in Rome and developed a monumental style. He introduced Saxony to the Nazarene art movement. The pictures in the Domed Hall are dedicated to the fine arts: crescent-shaped fields contain allegorical representations of painting, sculpture, music and architecture, each accompanied by two medallion images of "divine" exponents: Raphael and Jan van Eyck for painting, Phidias and Peter Vischer for sculpture, Wolfgang Amadeus Mozart and Giovanni Pierluigi da Palestrina for music and Dinocrates of Macedon and Erwin von Steinbach for architecture. Allegories of poetry, love and philosophy and the three Graces Aglaia, Euphrosyne and Thalia complete the sequence.

Situated immediately ahead of the Domed Hall is the Chinesisches Kaffeezimmer or Chinese Coffee Room, which was created in the 1890s. The room's most significant element was a panoramic Chinese tapestry on paper, created in the latter part of the 18th century in the Anthony or Seequa painting workshops in Canton in South China. The way this panoramic tapestry is presented at Pillnitz

opposite
Passage leading to the chapel, with busts of the rulers of Saxony

View looking towards the altar of the Catholic Chapel

is not faithful to its original shape and context – the sections have been separated and they are presented as panels on the wall in the wrong sequence, in combination with a bamboo framework and decorative porcelain on plasterwork consoles. This loose arrangement is held together by the art nouveau paintings in the ceiling coving. In this coffee room, which is still somewhat reminiscent of a baroque porcelain cabinet, Pillnitz displays a typical example of the historicist era: original Chinese art combined with European design to suit individual tastes.

One reaches the Catholic Court Chapel (10) from the Kuppelsaal by means of a long passage. The chapel is integrated into the castle complex, and is therefore represented only by certain symbolic structures: a small, squat bell tower with a golden cross and a characteristic church window. The Pillnitz palace chapel is a single-aisle room whose angled corners make it appear oval. It is given a quiet, solemn atmosphere by its paintings and by the restrained pattern of the wall and ceiling surfaces. The design is based on the Dresden Josephinenstift chapel, from which Schuricht borrowed the paired Corinthian pilasters and the entablature with an architrave, smooth frieze and console cornice which he uses to give the walls their structure. The entablature is interrupted above the gable-topped portal on the east side, leaving the small organ gallery, with its Jehmlich organ, exposed to view. The chapel's extravagant accoutrements also include a sarcophagus-like altar. On the altar, three golden tripod candlesticks stand on either side of the marble Sacrament niche. The altar painting above shows Mary sitting on a bank of cloud. Her right arm supports a naked, standing figure of the child Jesus, who winds his arm around her neck. The image is one of a type in which the child turns towards the mother and presses his cheek against hers tenderly, showing Mary as "Eleusa" (the merciful). Looking towards her are, on the right, Johannes Nepomuk, one of Bohemia's most important saints, and, on the left, Bishop Benno of Meissen. To one side of the altar is a wooden pulpit that can also be reached from the sacristy. The pulpit cover is decorated with a continuous golden egg-and-dart border, and is topped with a cross. The pulpit rests on a foliate console. The central church window has a glass painting, donated by court cook Christoph Schlein in 1902. It shows the mother of God enthroned, with the Christ child as the ruler of the world. The insignia indicate that Mary is the queen of heaven. The group also includes Albertus Magnus (circa 1200–1280) and Carl Borromäus (1538–1584), the namesakes of King Albert and Queen Carola.

Mural showing the "Presentation in the Temple".
Carl Christian Vogel von Vogelstein, 1819

The scenes from the life of Mary in the Catholic Chapel were painted by court painter Carl Christian Vogel von Vogelstein, who converted to

Catholicism in Rome in 1819 and was therefore in a good position to create a series of pictures which visualises both the private and public religious activities of the ruling house and the power of belief and of trust in God. The scenes are from the lives of Christ and Mary: "the Annunciation", "the Visitation", "the Adoration of the Shepherds", "the Presentation in the Temple", "the Flight into Egypt", "the Discovery in the Temple", "the Death of Mary", "the Ascension of Mary" and "the Crowning of Mary". The "Presentation in the Temple" is clearly intended for the royal chapel; in the background of the scene are six portraits of members of the royal family. Aside from King Friedrich August I, the figures, from left to right, are: his nephew, the future king Prince Friedrich August (1797–1854), his brother Prince Maximilian (1759–1838), Prince Johann's consort Amalie Auguste (1801–1877) with the king's great-nephew, the future King Albert (1828–1902) on her arm and the king's nephew, the prince and future King Johann (1801–1873). The mural is dated on the lower right-hand edge: "XXIV Octobr. MDCCCXXIX", although the painter did not complete his work until the 16th of December of the same year. The whole cycle demonstrates Vogel's desire to use art as an educating and elevating influence to strengthen beliefs. The power and confidence of the figures engaged in actions in Vogel's painting arise from his own religious affinities. He aims to give them the maximum impact through pure shapes that emphasise spiritual expression (very much in the spirit of the Nazarene movement) and a choice of colours determined by symbolic and emotional values. The pictures are intended to signify the warmth and sense of blessing that comes from belief in God. Aside from the depicted Biblical stories, deep emotions, devoted faith, trust in

God, omnipresent revelation and love of God and one's fellow men are the real themes of Vogelstein's paintings.

There are apartments for the clerics and for the castle administrators situated in the east part of the chapel wing, behind the stairwell. The kitchen wing is on the Elbe side. The royal court kitchen used to be housed in its basement. There were also a number of (generally smaller) kitchens intended for preparing tea or for serving individual storeys, and a larger kitchen in the cellars of the Upper Palace, but the main, central kitchen was in the New Palace. Schuricht's design for it was based on the old kitchen in the Renaissance Castle, destroyed in the fire. It is divided into a kitchen, a bakery and a roasting area, a spices pantry, storage rooms and an ice cellar; the kitchen accounts area and the silverware cabinet adjoined this

View of the Lilac Courtyard, with the trees in bloom

opposite

View of the kitchen section of the Royal Court Kitchen

area of the building toward the Kuppelsaal.

The Lilac Courtyard (11) lies between the two wings. The façade design is more autonomous here: it is strictly classicist, with Doric columns being a feature of the Kuppelsaal balcony in particular. The courtyard design is striking: in the mid-19th century, it was planted with over 100 Chinese lilac trees. Their twisted trunks have a particular charm.

The Guardhouse Building (12), erected in 1824 for the use of the guard company who had been transferred to Pillnitz, was clearly designed with more restraint, appropriately to its function, using neoclassical forms; it is sited in front of the chapel wing on the Borsberg side. As befits its function, its design features very restrained elements which nonetheless reference classicist forms. Further back, behind this building, is the former site of the

Kammergut (13), the state-run agricultural concern that replaced the estate farmlands. No agriculture takes place here today; the former stables and farm buildings are used by the State Office of the Environment, Agriculture and Geology, Saxony.

THE ENGLISH GARDEN AND ITS PAVILION

In 1778, Elector Friedrich August III bought the plot at the northwest end of the gardens, so that he could create the English Garden (14) there. It was laid out to appear as natural as possible; everything was to be brought together in a

seemingly random way, with no visible traces of the gardener's hand, to create a garden that was, like nature, seemingly created by God's own hand. Equipped with places to rest, this garden was entirely devoted to pleasure and to the quiet contemplation of an artificially arranged landscape: the new attitude that

marked the decline of architecture as the dominant symbol of absolutist power. The garden, which was probably designed by the elector himself, was walled; it was not intended to be a part of the wider landscape. Its internal structure was subdivided into so-called English boskets – hedged areas containing trees and perennials, penetrated by labyrinthine paths. In the centre was a clearing with a pond – on which many lines of sight converge – which still visually dominates the space today. On the north end of the pond, which contains an island lined with poplar trees to recall the famous memorial to the author and philosopher Jean-Jacques Rousseau (1712–

1778), is the English Pavilion (15), built by Johann Daniel Schade in 1780. It is based on the Tempietto of San Pietro at Montorio in Rome, built by Donato Bramante (1444–1514) circa 1502. Rather than being a copy of the Tempietto, however, it is a flexible interpretation that provides a suitable vantage point and resting place, making it more suitable for a landscaped garden.

The pavilion is a round two-storey building rising from a three-tiered substructure. Eight pairs of Ionic columns stand in front of the outer wall of the ground storey, supporting a classical entablature. A walkway, bordered by a cast-iron grille parapet, leads to the recessed upper storey. The tower's eight windows pointing in every direction of the compass (two of which are false windows) are a reference to the ancient Tower of the Winds in Athens. The interior was made oval in shape so that a staircase could be incorporated: the low step height, however, still

made it necessary to include an intermediate storey. The pavilion's interior has a startlingly cool elegance. The wall surfaces, which are clad in grey-green stucco marble, are decorated with white arabesques and with medallions surrounded by ornamental vines. The lower part of the wall is decorated with applied flat reliefs showing scenes from antiquity. It is the upper storey that defines the English Pavilion's function. This room is decorated almost entirely in white – only the wooden elements are decorated with scientifically accurate representations of butterflies, caterpillars and pupae, revealing that this room was a cabinet intended for study. The pictures are based on images from the standard work on entomology by August Johann Rösel von Rosenhof (1705–1759).

According to the standard work on gardens of the time – the "Theorie der Gartenkunst" by Christian Cay Lorenz Hirschfeld (1742–1792) – the English Pavilion is a study cabinet in a "noon garden" that verges on an "afternoon garden". The book's recommendations were followed to the letter: the correct selection of shade-giving trees to be planted around such a pavilion, cool water, and a secluded retreat from which one could watch the sun going down in the west amid wonderful natural scenery. The Friedrichsgrund, a nearby part of the Borsberg landscape situated outside the Castle Garden, is laid out in the style of an early, sentimental landscape garden, and is therefore to some degree a part of the English Garden's overall concept. Friedrich August I had a small hermitage built on the top of the Borsberg in 1775, and by the mid-1780s he had transformed the natural landscape into an open garden landscape by adding more small "beautifying" touches, including an artificial waterfall and an artificial Gothic ruin. Friedrichsgrund and Borsberg

Part of the Friedrichsgrund landscape

provided settings for court celebrations from then on, but they were also places of intimate contemplation for the nature-loving king.

THE DUTCH GARDEN AND THE PLANT HOUSES

Like the English part of the garden, the Dutch Garden (16) and its plant houses were the result of Friedrich August the Just's efforts to continue to develop Dresden's court gardens despite the depletion of Saxony's coffers following the Seven Year's War. Pillnitz

The Palm House in the Dutch Garden was chosen as the location for these garden projects partly because of its status as a summer residence: at Pillnitz, the elector himself oversaw the gardens. The purchasing of land for new gardens and the garden facilities built at Pillnitz were decided with scientific research in mind from the very beginning. For instance, a specialised nursery for North American trees and a conservatory for Mediterranean plants were incorporated into the English Garden.

Pillnitz' first heated greenhouses were built in the Dutch Garden in 1786, on the site where the Palm House stands today. The garden's name derives from the plants they contained, which originated mainly from Dutch colonies in South Africa and Australia. The original botanical facilities also contained an open-air area for raising per-

View of the central octagonal space in the Palm House

ennials. When King Friedrich August I died (in 1827), there were 4,305 plant species at Pillnitz. He had had his nephew, the future King Friedrich August II, trained in botany to enable him to continue the work he himself had started, earning the future ruler the nickname "the botanist on the royal throne of Saxony". During Friedrich August II's rule, the inventory of plants was expanded to include 16,000 species. After the early death of the king in 1854, his brother Johann became responsible for the collection. In addition to deciding that the collection should remain at Pillnitz, he gave orders for more greenhouses to be built, as more space was urgently needed for the increased number of specimens. Under the leadership of Hofbaumeister (court architect) Heinrich Eduard Hassler, the Palm House (17) – a cast iron skeleton construction that was highly modern for its age – was built. Its construction began in 1859 and was completed in 1861. The Palm House' octagonal main room rises impressively from the centre of this triple building, with its pyramidal roof making it appear like a glass crystal. Initially, it was only in this part of the structure that plants – primarily palms – were displayed all year round, with the adjoining sections used for overwintering plants and for propagating rare specimens. Today, the Palm House is a plant display house containing rare specimens of transplanted African and Australian flora. The selection and combination of the plants, as well as the design of the beds, is based on their distribution in natural ecosystems. The glasshouse complex is divided into cold and warm areas.

The Orangerie (18), which is situated below the Palm House, owes its conversion into a dedicated plant house to Johann's successor on the throne of Saxony, King Albert. The baroque Ringrennen building built by Matthäus Daniel Pöppelmann in 1725, an eight-sided building with a mansard roof, was first used as an orangery in 1799, during the reign of Friedrich August the Just, although after the fire of 1818 destroyed the Hoftheater (court theatre), the building would occasionally also be used for theatrical performances. Today, we are reminded of the building's original purpose by the sporting symbols on the front and rear central doors: an arrow, a ring and balls are arranged around a coat-of-arms cartouche bearing the initials AR (August Rex). The building once housed a carousel on which players would "tilt with lances at rings". In 1879, König Albert had the building extended by adding two long side wings, with an overall length of almost 100 metres. The building is lit by large round-arch windows along

The Orangerie, consisting of the former Ringrennen building and adjacent wings

its south side, allowing the plants to be stacked high in a tiered arrangement. The extension became necessary after the Orangerie parterre terrace in the Dresdner Zwinger had to be abandoned, meaning that the 170 trees that remained from the "bloom" of orangeries in Dresden needed a new winter shelter, which was supplied either at Pillnitz or at Grosssedlitz. The mobile Camellia House (19), which protects the Pillnitz camellia in the winter months, stands next to the Orangerie.

In the final third of the 19th century, the playing fields in front of the Orangerie – a relic from the age of baroque festivities – were abandoned, and the first North American conifers were planted in what is today the Conifer Grove

The Pillnitz camellia

The Pillnitz camellia is the oldest plant of its kind north of the Alps, if not the oldest in Europe. This woody plant belongs to the same family as the tea plant, and is native to eastern and southeast Asia. The first camellia japonica plants are said to have reached England as early as the 17th century, introduced by East India Company merchants. The Pillnitz camellia was presumably brought to Pillnitz from Asia as a young plant in the 1780s, possibly by the Swedish botanist Karl Peter Thunberg (1743–1828) The court gardener initially planted it in a tub.

In 1801, the gardener planted it in the position where it can still be admired today. It was initially covered over with straw and raffia in winter to protect it from the cold, and was later surrounded with a wooden structure which could be dismantled and reassembled, and which was required to be heated. When the camellia's greenhouse burned down in January 1905 due to overheating, the water used to extinguish the fire froze at minus 20 degrees, covering the plant and keeping it from freezing, with the result that it put out new shoots in the

The Pillnitz camellia in its protective house

The Pillnitz camellia in bloom

spring of the same year. In 1992, the camellia was given a glass protective housing with moveable parts, with the temperature, ventilation, shade and humidity within regulated by a climate computer. This structure is 13.2 metres high and weighs 54 tonnes, and the air space within is 1,864 cubic metres. In the warm months, the structure is moved to stand beside the camellia, which stands in the open air of the Castle Park. The plant has reached a size of 8.90 metres, a diameter of 11 metres and a circumference of over 33 metres. Every year, thousands of its single, crimson blossoms appear to delight visitors, often while snow is still on the ground.

(20) conifer collection. The avenue of lime trees in front of the Orangerie building was also removed at this time.

THE CHINESE GARDEN AND ITS PAVILION

The Chinese Garden (21), which adjoins the Orangerie and the Palm House on the northeast side, is another of the extensions to Pillnitz's gardens made for botanical purposes by Friedrich August the Just. It was the result of an experiment; hardy trees, chosen to suit the garden's design, were brought together to create a landscaped garden. The site of the garden was purchased in 1790; it already contained the pond, which had previously been used as a reservoir to supply the Pleasure

The interior of the Chinese Pavilion, featuring real Chinese landscapes

opposite
The Chinese Pavilion

Garden fountain. The garden was named after the pavilion of the same name, which was built by Christian Friedrich Schuricht at the northern end in 1804.

The Chinese Pavilion (22) consists of a square main room adjoined by three small rooms on the north side. The main room is overlaid with an open vault that leaves a second ceiling exposed to view. Four columns in front of each of the garden-facing sides of the pavilion support a stepped tent roof whose edges have a concave curve, with additional console-type squared timbers also supporting the roof. The extension of the gardens and the construction of the pavilion around 1804 took place during a revival of the *chinoiserie* style. Here an attempt was made to emulate Chinese architecture and original building techniques, rather than merely to create an Oriental impression as with the Riverside Palace and the Upper Palace. The standard reference work of the age was William Chambers' "Designs of Chinese Buildings", published in 1757, which contained copper-etched reproductions of exemplary construction forms observed by the author in China. Head architect Christian Friedrich Schuricht took these as his model, but was unaware how inaccurately Chambers had recorded the ancient traditional loadbearing structures of the buildings. As a consequence, he was unable to dispense with walls as load-bearing elements. The Chinese Pavilion that was ultimately constructed appeared faithful to the drawings when seen from the outside, but could not be considered an authentic reproduction of the traditional Chinese building technique. The design of its interior, containing eight painted Chinese architectural landscapes created by Johann Ludwig Giesel (1747–1814), is extraordinary. What is really remarkable about these paintings is that they are based on real examples of Chinese architecture, some of which still exist today – such as the Beihai park to the north of Peking's Forbidden City and the Putuo Zongcheng temple in Chengde. The models for these landscapes were taken from the reports of an embassy sent by King George III of Great Britain to the court of the Emperor of China in 1792/93. Draughtsman William Alexander had created a record of this journey, and the painter used his work as a basis for his wall paintings.

It is worth walking back to the Elbe from the Chinese Garden. This provides a magical conclusion to your visit to the Pillnitz Castle and Park.

opposite
Statue of Flora by the sculptur Wolf von Hoyer
in the Dutch Garden, 1870

CHRONOLOGY

circa 1400 Pillnitz, presumably a fiefdom of the Burgrave of Dohna, belongs to the parish of Dohna until 1539.

1403 Heinrich von Karas is made lord of the manor of Pillnitz.

1486–1569 Pillnitz is held by the Ziegler family.

1569–1640 The Pillnitz estate is owned by the von Loss family. They have a four-wing Renaissance Castle built.

1578 A fruit and kitchen garden is mentioned for the first time.

1594–1596 The Castle Church is built.

1640–1694 The estate of Pillnitz is owned by the Bünau family.

1694 Elector Johann Georg IV of Saxony acquires the estate of Pillnitz.

1707 Pillnitz is given to Anna Constantia, countess of Cosel. She has the Hedge Garden laid out.

1718 August the Strong takes possession of Pillnitz.

1720–1730 The Riverside Palace, the Upper Palace, the Pleasure Garden, the Elbe open staircase, the Temple of Venus, the Ringrennen building and the Games Garden are created.

1778–1791 Wings are added to the Water Palace and the Upper Palace, and the gardens are expanded by the addition of the English Garden and the Chinese Garden.

1818–1826 The New Palace and the Guardhouse Building are built.

1859–1861 The Palm House is built.

1863–1864	The Guard Houses near the ha-ha are built.
1874	The Ringrennen building is expanded to create the Orangerie.
1874–1880	The conifer garden is laid out in the former games garden.
1924	Pillnitz Castle and the Castle Park are taken over by the state.
1952	The castle and its park are transferred to the City of Dresden.
1963	The Museum for Arts and Crafts opens.
1992	The glazed protective housing for the camellia is built.
1993	The Free State of Saxony takes responsibility for Pillnitz Castle and its park.
1996	The visitors' centre in the Guardhouse Building next to the New Palace opens.
2003	Pillnitz Castle and Park become part of Staatliche Schlösser, Burgen und Gärten Sachsen.
2006	The Castle Museum opens in the New Palace.
2009	The Palm House reopens.

SELECTED LITERATURE

Anke Fröhlich: Barocke Spiele im Schlosspark Pillnitz. In: Jahrbuch der Staatlichen Schlösser, Burgen und Gärten Sachsen 12 (2004), pp. 80–93.

Gottfried Ganssauge: Die Geschichte des Pillnitzer Schlosses. Dresden 1932.

Kurt Gliemeroth and Roland Puppe: Schlosspark Pillnitz. Ein dendrologischer Führer. Leipzig 2000.

Hans-Günther Hartmann: Pillnitz – Schloss, Park und Dorf. Weimar 1981.

Igor A. Jenzen: Schloss und Park Pillnitz. Berlin 1998.

Hans F. Kammeyer: Der Schlossgarten zu Dresden-Pillnitz. Berlin 1957.

Fritz Löffler: Schloss und Park Pillnitz. Dresden 1951.

Heinrich Magirius: Zur Entstehungsgeschichte des Schlosses Pillnitz und seiner Fassadenbemalung. In: Denkmale in Sachsen. Ihre Erhaltung und Pflege in den Bezirken Dresden, Karl-Marx-Stadt, Leipzig and Cottbus. Weimar 1978, pp. 249–278.

Heinrich Magirius: Pillnitz, Schloss und Park. Leipzig 1994.

Stefanie Melzer: Früh 6 Uhr begaben sich Seine Churfürstliche Durchlaucht nach der Eremitage … Zur Ausgestaltung von Friedrichsgrund und Borsberghängen im Stil des frühen sentimentalen Landschaftsgartens. In Jahrbuch der Staatlichen Schlösser, Burgen und Gärten Sachsen 14 (2006), pp. 173–184.

Stefanie Melzer: In den Fussstapfen Lennés. Friedrich August der Gerechte und die Botanik. In: Jahrbuch der Staatlichen Schlösser, Burgen und Gärten Sachsen 15 (2008), pp. 120–129.

August von Minckwitz: Geschichte von Pillnitz vom Jahre 1403 an. Dresden 1893.

Hans-Joachim Neidhardt: Schloss Pillnitz. Dresden 1980.

Jens Scheffler: Die Nachahmung der Natur, durch Kunst und Ordnung verherrlicht. Zur Geschichte des Englischen Gartens im Schlosspark Pillnitz. In Jahrbuch der Staatlichen Schlösser, Burgen und Gärten Sachsen 10 (2002), pp. 20–30.

Ines Täuber: Die Weinligzimmer im Bergpalais des Pillnitzer Schlosses. In: Jahrbuch der Staatlichen Schlösser, Burgen und Gärten Sachsen 12 (2004), pp. 114–129.

Juliane Thiele: Pillnitz als Sommerresidenz und die Wohnausstattung des Wasser- und Bergpalais am Ende des 18. Jahrhunderts. In: Jahrbuch der Staatlichen Schlösser, Burgen und Gärten Sachsen 14 (2006), pp. 78–89.

Dirk Welich: Der Chinesische Garten und Pavillon in Pillnitz. Dresden 2001.

Dirk Welich: Der Englische Pavillon in Pillnitz. In Jahrbuch der Staatlichen Schlösser, Burgen und Gärten Sachsen 11 (2003), pp. 22–28.

Dirk Welich und Birgit Finger: Die Katholische Kapelle im Schloss Pillnitz. Dresden 2002.

SERVICE

How to find us

Pillnitz Castle is sited on the eastern outskirts of Dresden, directly on the Elbe. The castle complex is well served by public transport, by Sächsische Dampfschiffahrt steamers or by car. It is also possible to cycle along the Elbe cycle path and cross the river by ferry to the castle.

Autobahn access is via the A4 (Dresden-Hellerau or Dresden-Altstadt exit towards Pillnitz) or the A17 (Pirna exit, then on towards Radeberg, Graupa exit, on to Pillnitz).

Public parking is available in Leonardo-da-Vinci Strasse, and for coaches by the "Alte Wache"; a limited number of handicapped parking spaces are available at the ferry landing stage.

Pillnitz Castle is accessible by public transport on the no. 63 bus to Leonardo-da-Vinci-Strasse or Pillnitzer Platz, on the left bank of the Elbe on the no. 88 bus or no. 2 tram to the terminus in each case, and then by ferry across the Elbe, or from Pirna on the P bus route to Leonardo-da-Vinci-Strasse or Pillnitzer Platz.

Opening times

The park is open all year round
April to October
Admission fee is charged
Mon.–Sun.   09.00 to 20.00

November to March
Admission fee is charged
Sat./Sun.   10.00 to 17.00

Botanical greenhouses
Camellia House
Mid February to mid April

Palm House
April to October   10.00 to 18.00
November to March   10.00 to 16.00

Castle Museum in the New Palace
Museum for Arts and Crafts in the Riverside Palace and Upper Palace
May to October
Tues.–Sun.   10.00 to 18.00

Service

Guided tours and group arrangements can be organised all the year round with advance notification. Dates for public guided tours, events and concerts can be found in the annual events calendar. Various rental offers and also overnight stay facilities are available in the Castle Park itself.
Guided tours are offered regularly at weekends from November to April in the Castle Museum.

Contact

Schlösser und Gärten Dresden
Schloss & Park Pillnitz
August-Böckstiegel-Strasse 2
01326 Dresden

Telephone 0351 / 2613260
Telefax 0351 / 2613280

pillnitz@schloesserland-sachsen.de
www.schlosspillnitz.de
www.schloesserland-sachsen.de

Picture credits

Staatliche Schlösser, Burgen und Gärten Sachsen, head office, picture archive, and Schlösser und Gärten Dresden, Schloss und Park Pillnitz, picture archive: pp. 12, 21, 32/33, 34, 35 top, 36, photograph Gabriele Goers (Hanke; front cover), photographs Klaus-Dieter Weber (pp. 2/3, 60), Hans-Peter Klut (p. 5 top), Herbert Boswank (p. 5 bottom), Frank Höhler (front flap outside, pp. 9, 14, 23, 24/25, 31, 35 bottom, 37, 38, 40, 43, 44, 46, 48, 49, 50, 51, 52, 53, 55, 56, 57, 58, 62, 65), postcard of a collotype by the Dorn & Merfeld press (p. 17), Thomas Ebischbach (p. 26), Matthias Lüttich (p. 61 top and bottom), Jürgen Karpinski (p. 65), model perspektive.grün (p. 29), pingundpong (back flap inside), buero4 (front flap inside), Dirk Laubner (back cover); Landesamt für Denkmalpflege Sachsen, plan collection (p. 15); Sächsische Landesbibliothek, Staats- und Universitätsbibliothek Dresden (SLUB), Deutsche Fotothek, (pp. 4, 6/7, 8, 18, 41); Staatliche Kunstsammlungen Dresden, Gemäldegalerie Alte Meister, photograph Deutsche Fotothek (p. 11), Kunstgewerbemuseum, photograph Jürgen Karpinski (p. 27)

Imprint

Front cover image: Pillnitz Castle, Upper Palais
Back cover image: Pillnitz Castle and Park from the southeast

Bibliographical information of the Deutsche Nationalbibliothek
The Deutsche Nationalbibliothek lists this publication in the Deutsche Nationalbibliografie; detailed bibliographical information can be found on the internet at http://dnb.d-nb.de.

ISBN 978-3-361-00672-0

© 2012 by Edition Leipzig of Seemann Henschel GmbH & Co. KG,
Staatliche Schlösser, Burgen und Gärten Sachsen and the authors
www.edition-leipzig.de

Cover design, layout and typesetting: Gudrun Hommers, Berlin
Editing: Matthias Donath
Picture editing: Miriam Röther
Translation: Michael Robinson, London
Proof-reading: Catherine Hughes, Berlin
Production: Thomas Flach
Repro: Bild1Druck, Berlin
Printing and binding: Stürtz, Würzburg

Printed in Germany

Printed on ageing-resistant paper using chlorine-free pulp

More books on castles in Saxony:

Matthias Donath /
Dirk Welich
**Der Zwinger
zu Dresden**
48 pages, 30 illustrations
ISBN 978-3-361-00668-3

Matthias Donath /
Dirk Welich
**The Dresden
Zwinger**
48 pages, 30 illustrations
ISBN 978-3-361-00669-0

Matthias Donath /
Roland Puppe
**Der Große Garten
in Dresden**
48 pages, 30 illustrations
ISBN 978-3-361-00677-5

Wiebke Glöckner /
Ingolf Gräßler
**Burg Mildenstein
in Leisnig**
48 pages, 30 illustrations
ISBN 978-3-361-00675-1

Simona Schellenberger /
Falk Schulze
Burg Gnandstein
48 pages, 30 illustrations
ISBN 978-3-361-00676-8

Matthias Donath /
André Thieme
**Albrechtsburg
Meissen**
72 pages, 40 illustrations
ISBN 978-3-361-00662-1

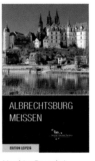

Matthias Donath /
André Thieme
**Albrechtsburg
Meissen** English Edition
72 pages, 40 illustrations
ISBN 978-3-361-00664-5

Matthias Donath /
André Thieme
Kloster Altzella
48 pages, 30 illustrations
ISBN 978-3-361-00663-8

Matthias Donath /
Peter Wunderwald
Schloss Nossen
48 pages, 30 illustrations
ISBN 978-3-361-00661-4

Matthias Donath
**Sachsens
schönste Schlösser,
Burgen und Gärten**
128 pages, 96 illustrations
ISBN 978-3-361-00667-6